A Conflict on the Church and the Sacraments

How Rome and the Reformation differed at Regensburg in 1541

Steven Paas

Kachere Series, Zomba 2006

Copyright © 2006 Steven Paas

All rights reserved. No part of this publication may be reproduced, stored in a retrieval system, or transmitted in any form or by any means, electronic, mechanical, photocopying, recording or otherwise, without prior permission by the author.

Published by: Kachere Series, P.O. Box 1037, Zomba, Malawi

ISBN: 99908-76-64-9
ISBN-13: 978-99908-76-64-2
Kachere Text no. 26

The Kachere Series is represented outside Africa by:

African Books Collective Oxford (orders@africanbookscollective.com)
Michigan State University Press East Lansing (msupress@msu.edu)

Layout and cover graphics: Willem Hendrik Paas

Cover illustration: The City of Regensburg

Printed by: Lightning Source

Kachere Series
P.O. Box 1037,
Zomba, Malawi
kachere@globemw.net
www.sdnp.org.mw/kachereseries

This book is part of the Kachere Series, a range of books on religion, culture and society in Malawi.

Other Kachere/ Mvunguti Books by Steven Paas:

Digging Out the Ancestral Church: Researching and Communicating Church History

Chikonzedwe cha Mpingo: Zosintha Zazikulu za Uzimu 1500-1650

Mpingo Wakale: Mbiri ya m' zaka za 1-500

English – Chichewa/ Chinyanja Dictionary

Chichewa/ Chinyanja – English Dictionary

A Conflict on Authority in the Early African Church: Augustine of Hippo and the Donatists

From Galilee to the Atlantic: A History of the Church in Africa
Kaphunziridwe ka Baibulo - A Guide for Bible Study Groups

English Lessons from the Bible – Maphunziro a chiNgerezi m'Baibulo

The Faith Moves South: A History of the Church in Africa

The Kachere Series is the publications arm of the Department of Theology and Religious Studies of the University of Malawi.

Series Editors: J.C. Chakanza, F.L. Chingota, Klaus Fiedler, P.A. Kalilombe, I.S. Mahommad, Fulata Moyo, Martin Ott

Contents

Preface 5
Chapter 1 6
Reform, Reformation, Restitution 6
   a. The Objective of this Study 6
   b. The Political and Ecclesiastical Situation 7
   c. The Disputation as a Means to make Change 10
   d. Hagenau, Worms, Regensburg 13
Chapter 2 16
The Extremes Meet 16
   a. Four Aspects 16
   b. Contarini about the *Confessio Augustana* 16
   c. Gropper's *Enchiridion* 20
   d. Bucer and the *Leipzig Draft for Re-union* 24
Chapter 3 29
Rapprochement and Separation 29
   a. Regensburg 1541 29
   b. Teaching on Grace 30
   c. Ecclesiology 33
   d. Teaching on the Sacraments 35
   e. Practical Issues 36
Chapter 4 38
Deeper Unity of Dogma 38
   a. Church and Sacraments 38
   b. Deeper Unity not Appreciated 39

Preface

According to popular thought, it was the doctrine of *Justification* that divided Rome and the Reformation in the 16th century. However, in a wider theological concept the real breaking point was not the doctrine of Justification, but the issue of *Church and Sacraments*. The author drew this conclusion from his study of the last dramatic meeting between representatives of Rome and the Reformation in the German city of Regensburg in the year 1541. The *Regensburg Disputation* was the last official encounter between Roman Catholicism and Protestantism for a very long time. Only in the second half of the 20th century, churches of the Reformation, mainly the Anglicans and the Lutherans, started dialogue with the Roman Catholic Church, after the *Ecumenical Movement*, and the *Second Vatican Council* had paved the way for this. Still, questions of sacramental and ecclesiastical power proved more divisive than the belief of justification by faith. This situation was reflected by publications of the results of a Conference on Baptism, Eucharist and Ministry, organised by the *Faith and Order* Committee of the *World Council of Churches*, in the Peruvian capital Lima in 1982.[1]

    The issue of Church and Sacraments has remained important, also in the African context. Theology in African perspective needs an *Ecclesiology* which rests in Scripture and which therefore is significant to the specific features of African culture. May this representation of the thoughts developed by the participants of the *Regensburg Disputation* in 1541, be helpful in today's discussion.

    I thank Rev. Stephen McCracken, Fr. Michael McGuckian, and Dr. Klaus Fiedler for reading this text and helping me to improve it.

Zomba, 2006
Steven Paas

---

[1] *Baptism, Eucharist and Ministry: Statements of the Faith and Order Committee of the World Council of Churches*, Lima, Peru, 1982; Max Thurian (ed.), *BEM: Official Response to the Baptism, Eucharist and Ministry Text*, Geneva: World Council of Churches, from 1986.

Chapter 1

Reform, Reformation, Restitution

a. The Objective of this Study

In 1957 Hans Küng in his book *Rechtfertigung*[2] (Justification) wanted to show that the historical rift between Protestantism and Roman Catholicism has been much less determined by the doctrine of justification than many have thought.

Küng drew this conclusion after having studied the statements of the *Council of Trent* (1545-1563) on justification. In his view these statements, especially the one in Sessio VI, could be explained in a Protestant sense. This is a remarkable conclusion. Karl Barth († 1968) was of the opinion that Küng well described the Protestant teaching of justification, at least in agreement with the way Barth himself saw Protestantism. But Barth doubted whether Kung had really understood the Decretals of Trent on justification, especially having in mind the strong condemnation by Trent of anyone who holds the Protestant view.

Karl Barth (1886-1968), one of the most influential Protestant theologians of the 20th century, mainly through his Commentary on Paul's Epistle to the Romans (1919), and the systematic exposition of his theology in Church Dogmatics (1967).

In this study we will investigate what has been the main bone of contention between Rome and the Reformation. However, we will not look at the deliberations and pronouncements of Trent, but at the period just before that Church Council, when Roman Catholic dogma was not yet as strictly formulated as in the period from Trent onwards. We are investigating the religious Disputations of the 1530s and early 1540s, especially the one in

---

[2] H.Küng, *Rechtfertigung: Die Lehre Karl Barths und eine Katholische Besinnung*, Einsiedeln: Johannes Verlag, 1957.

Regensburg in 1541. Which were the main reasons why the Protestant and the Roman Catholic participants in the Disputations finally separated?

b. The Political and Ecclesiastical Situation

Peace in Europe has always depended very much on the situation in Germany. The re-unification of West and East Germany in 1990 has given Germany and the whole of Europe stability after a long history of integration and disintegration since the *Habsburg Empire* of Charles V († 1558). In that historical process the role of the Church changed, though it has not lost its

A view of the city of Trent in the Adige River valley in North Italy, where during the period 1545-1563, in discontinuous sessions, a Roman Catholic Church Council took place, that formulated its opposition to the Protestant Reformation, condemning the Reformed views of Justification, of the Church and of the Sacraments.

importance. For a long time the feudal organisation of State and Church was the cornerstone of the unity of the Empire. In Charles V's time the foundations of imperial and ecclesiastical unity were still functioning, but they showed dangerous cracks. Territorial princes and city magistrates had grown more powerful. Movements of ecclesiastical Reform had become influential. This undermined the supremacy of the Emperor and of the Pope.

The protests against abuses in the Church had become sharper and more subversive as the Pope systematically postponed a Church Council that could deal with the main grievances. Many were not satisfied anymore with just a face-lift of the Church. Encouraged by Humanism that pretended to have rediscovered the beauty and purity of Antiquity, they wanted a Restitution of the Church after the model of the Early Church. In this movement there were two wings. One was called the Religious or Biblical Humanism. It did not intend to break the unity of the Church of Rome. It had developed under the influence of the *devotion moderna* in The Netherlands and North Germany. In the beginning this wing of Humanism, represented by Erasmus of Rotterdam († 1536) and others, was sympathetic to the Lutheran Reformation. This Biblical Humanism was different from the Humanism in South Germany and Italy that was directly connected to the secularising movement of Renaissance and its interest in classical pagan Antiquity.[3] Both wings of Humanism were characterised by tolerance, freedom of dogmatic position, emphasis on the teaching of morality, and an interest in the world of Antiquity. They differed by being more or less oriented on Christian faith and Biblical revelation. Both wings were joined by quite a number of clergy. These priests thought that purification of the Church would give back to Rome its old splendour. Both wings of Humanism also produced the theologians and politicians that would take part in the Religious Disputations.[4]

Martin Luther (1483-1546), the Reformer at Wittenberg, personally participated in Disputations with Roman Catholic theologians like Cajetan and Eck, and indirectly he influenced the meetings at Hagenau, Worms and Regensburg.

The Reformation Movement was related to Religious Humanism, yet it was different. With Religious Humanism it shared a great interest in the Early Church. But its criterion was deeper. Restitution of the Early Church it considered basically impossible. History cannot be repeated, and should not be repeated, for this would mean repeating the degeneration that had already crept in. The Church Fathers were not of one mind; that is why we cannot copy them. The Church has to be thoroughly reformed. The sole normative is the Word of God. Those elements of the Church of history and of today that are in

---

[3] W. Lipgen, *Johannes Gropper und die Anfänge der katholischen Reform in Deutschland*, Munster: Aschendorffsche Verlagsbuchhandlung, 1951, pp. 21 ff, 39.
[4] Cf. J. Lortz, *Die Reformation in Deutschland*, volume 2, pp. 213 ff.

accordance to the Bible have to be connected to and used. This was de position of the Reformation.

Humanism and Reformation shared a desire for change, yet they were different. Humanism emphasised the need for removing abuses and for purification in the realm of ethics and morality. The Reformation also wanted this, but it first of all looked for the foundation of change. The Church did not only fail because of unfaithfulness to the Church Fathers and lack of sanctification. The deepest reason for Reformation was that the Church had failed to understand that it can only live by grace. This failure was followed by a distortion of sanctification.

In various ways the message of the Reformation was spread. Unfortunately the Church of the Middle Ages did not accept this powerful attempt of Reformation from within. Eventually Rome was only prepared to allow a number of practical changes; basically it remained immovably unchanged. This had to lead to a break.

The 16th century schism in the Church of the West had aspects of a tragedy. In the Council of Trent it would become irreversible. Before that time during the religious disputations men belonging to both opposing parties had hoped that schism could be prevented. These men were not the ecclesiastical leaders in Rome and Wittenberg. In the 1530s the rift between Luther and the Curia had already become wide and deep. Besides, there was the increasing contradiction between the Protestant princes, united in the *Schmalkaldic League* (1531), and the Roman Catholic princes. The one group tried to become more independent from the central powers of the Habsburg Empire and the other group tried to regain their control over the Empire.

Desiderius Erasmus of Rotterdam (1466-1536), a Humanist scholar who helped to pave the way for the Reformation, but remained loyal to the Church of Rome. He contributed to the climate in which theologians from both sides could try to reach a mutual understanding.

The schism was especially painful to those who recognised one another as members of the Body of Christ. Many of these people were touched by the harmony ideals of Religious Humanism. Although they belonged to different sides, they felt solidarity with one another. This was most apparent in those representatives of Rome and of the Reformation, who on the one hand wanted to keep their own identity, yet on the other hand were prepared to make as many concessions as possible for the sake of unity. They were influenced by Humanist motives of unity and peace, but they did not intend to sacrifice allegiance to their own party. At the same time, however, they were ready to formulate and interpret their own principles in such a way that the other party might recognise them or even agree to them. These humanistically coloured theologians on both sides were not many. Their objective was maintaining the unity and catholicity of the Church, and the execution of inward and outward reforms. In German they were called *Verständigungstheologen*, which means theologians who tried to reach mutual understanding.

In the 1530s the leaders of the Habsburg Empire apparently realised that these theologians could play a useful role in the attempts of the Emperor to keep the German part of his Empire together under Habsburg authority. The existence of the Empire was at stake because of external threats by France and by the Turks. In order to ward off these dangers, the Emperor needed a united Germany. In the first place this required religious unity.

c. The Disputation as a Means to make Change

The Emperor intervened in the current political and ecclesiastical situation. First he opted for peaceful means. He took the initiative for theologians of the two parties to meet for Disputation. This was not a new thing. Since the 12th century the method of Disputation had been used as a means for taking decisions and for initiating changes. In the beginning the Disputations were merely academic, directed at finding answers to questions in scholarly disputes. In 1519 at Leipzig this method was used when Reformer Martin Luther († 1546) had a discussion with Johann Eck († 1543). After that governments of cities and territories started to organise religious Disputations. Participants were challenged to decide in favour or against the Reformation, and the authorities used these meetings in the process of decision making.[5]

At the Diet of Augsburg in 1530 for the first time the method of religious Disputation was officially recognised at imperial level. In his *Confessio Augustana* Philipp Melanchthon († 1560) made concessions to the Roman Catholic party. A way of reconciliation seemed to be open. But the Roman Catholic Estates rejected this Protestant creed. After the publication of

---

[5] Marion Hollerbach, *Das Religionsgespräch als Mittel der konfessionellen und politischen Auseiandersetzung im Deutschland des 16. Jahrhunderts*, Frankfurt am Main: Peter Lang, 1982, pp. 1-81.

Melanchthon's subsequent *Apology* the parties were again opposed to one another like before. But that was not the end of the matter. In subsequent years conciliatory members in both parties would continue to exert themselves in attempts to reconcile Protestant and Roman Catholic stances. Here is an introduction to three of their writings, which played an important role in the discussions.

Emperor Charles V (1500-1558) of the Habsburg Empire, who for mainly political reasons, took the initiative for theologians of the Protestant and the Roman Catholic parties to meet for Disputation.

One of the delegates at the Diet of Augsburg was the Venetian theologian Gasparo Contarini († 1542). At that time he did not yet belong to the clergy. Five years later the Pope would elevate him to the position of Cardinal, and as such he would play an important role in the decisive stages of the theological Disputations. Contarini's *Confutatio*, commenting on what happened in Augsburg, was at least giving hope for future meetings.[6] In Augsburg there was also Johannes Gropper († 1559), a priest from the Archbishopric of Cologne. Educated in the school of Erasmus, Gropper belonged to the group of Reform-minded clergy. To him the Diet in Augsburg became a turning point that eventually made him to be a convinced defender of Rome. But in this hopeful period of religious Disputations, just like Contarini, he was prepared to do the utmost in making concessions to the opposing party. He showed this in his *Enchiridion* of 1538. Finally, he was made a Cardinal.[7] The third influential writing that we will discuss is of Protestant origin. It was the *Draft for Re-union* made at Leipzig in 1539, mainly by the Strasbourg Reformer Martin Bucer († 1551).[8] The important position of this document

---

[6] H. Jedin, *Kardinal Contarini als Kontroverstheologe*. Herausgabe Katholisches Leben und Kämpfen im Zeitalter der Glaubensspaltung. Vereinschriften der Gesellschaft zur Herausgabe des Corpus Catholoricum, Munster: Aschendorffsche Verlagsbuchhandlung, 1949, pp. 19-49

[7] For a discussion of the *Enchiridion*, see: Lipgen, *Gropper*, 67-103.

[8] *Leipziger Reunionsentwurf* (Leipzig Draft for Re-union). The text is to be found in: L. Cardauns, Zur Geschichte der kirchlichen Unions- und Reformbestrebungen von 1538 bis 1542. Bibliothek des kgl. Preussischen Historischen Instituts in Rom, Volume V; Rom: Verlag Von Loescher (W. Regensburg, 1910, pp. 85-108. According to Cardauns (p. 9) the text is to a great extent similar to Bucer's writing, *Ein ungefärlich Bedenken ...* (1545), which probably contains a summary of the discussion between Bucer, Witzel, Fachs and perhaps Melanchthon, about the proposals of Carlowitz.

needs to be indicated briefly.

By the end of the 1530s the Emperor was ready to allow representatives of religious Humanism a series of Disputations on the conflict between Protestants and Roman Catholics in his Empire, without direct involvement of the Pope and the Curia. The Emperor created a favourable political climate for these meetings. In 1539 he concluded an armistice with the Protestant princes, called *Frankfurter Anstand*. The time seemed to be ripe for the Emperor's initiative for religious peace. Some months earlier, in January 1539, in the Roman Catholic part of Saxony a religious Disputation had taken place. This Disputation had not led to complete agreement between the parties, yet it gave hope for fruitful continuation of this kind of theological negotiations. The Saxon Chancellor Georg Carlowitz had arranged meetings between e.g. the Strasbourg Reformer Martin Bucer and Georg Witzel, a theologian who once belonged to the followers of Martin Luther. Witzel had returned to the Roman Catholic Church, but he had kept his independent Humanist views.⁹ Carlowitz was of the opinion that the Curia in Rome had made the Church into a prostitute and should be excluded from the Disputations. He intended to reach an agreement of 'lay' people, founded on the teaching of the Early Church that would be accepted by all the German princes,1 before addressing the Emperor.¹⁰ Many were worried that the Emperor, together with France and the Pope, would re-impose the ecclesiastical authority of Rome on the whole of society. The Emperor had to be made to change his mind. A plan of re-union was supposed to prevent the Emperor from executing his plan. One of the participating theologians was Philipp Melanchthon, Luther's able assistant. Against his will he was drawn into this by Martin Bucer, who undoubtedly was the most influential disputant on the Protestant side. The *Leipzig Draft* (further *L.D.*) was the product of the

Philipp Melanchthon (1497-1560), Luther's younger friend and assistant, wrote the first well organised presentation of Reformed doctrine, Loci Communes (1521. He was the main author of the Augsburg Confession (1530). He personally participated in the Disputation of Regensburg 1541, and in preparatory meetings.

---

⁹ See Lortz, *Die Reformation*, volume 2, pp. 220 ff. for an extensive description of the life and significance of Georg Witzel.
¹⁰ Cardauns, *Zur Geschichte*, p.4.

discussions, of which Bucer was at least the main writer. This document would influence the development of thought at subsequent disputations. Through its effect, imperial policy had definitely taken an interest in the idea of reaching agreement by theological negotiations. Especially Bucer would play an important role in attempts to realise this.

d. Hagenau, Worms, Regensburg

The Habsburg rulers tried to strengthen their plan of re-union by initiating a meeting of Roman Catholic and Protestant *Estates* in Hagenau. The organisers decided to take the *Confessio Augustana* and the *Apology* as starting points for the negotiations. The second round of these discussions of *Estates* took place in Worms, where the participating theologians began their deliberations. The Emperor nominated the chairman, Granvella, an Erasmian tactician. By that time members of the Curia at Rome were very worried because of the imperial politics, because they felt excluded. That is why they sent a representative, Campeggio. The most important event in the meeting at Worms was a discussion between Melanchthon and Eck which resulted in some agreement as to the doctrine of original sin. But Granvella was not blinded by this small success. He realised that with the Protestant *Confessio Augustana* as starting point, there would be no really meaningful agreement between the parties. Therefore, already before the end of the conference he started secret discussions that were to lead to the acceptance of a different and more promising foundation for the negotiations. Gropper and Bucer belonged to the participants in these secret meetings. In these two meetings of able representatives of the conciliatory 'middle party' readiness to concessions was joined to principled tenacity. Gropper's *Enchiridion*, added and changed by Bucer, was used for making a draft text. First it was called the *Worms Draft* (Wormser Entwurf), and eventually it would bear the name of *Regensburg Book* (Regensburger Buch). It is not a creed like the *Confessio Augustana*, but a collection of disputed points, worked out in a proposed text, that was hoped to be acceptable for both parties.

Martin Bucer or Butzer (1491-1551), Reformer at Strasbourg, was the leading participant on the Protestant side of the Disputation at Regensburg, and of the meetings in preparation to it.

Then followed a period of diplomatic activities, of trying to get the parties to support this approach. Luther rejected the proposed text. But the Emperor decided to make this text the foundation for the religious Disputations at the Diet of Regensburg. The promising leading participants in the previous discussions were nominated as *collocutors* of the Regensburg meetings. The collocutors on the Roman Catholic side were Gropper, Eck and Pflug, and those on the Protestant side were Bucer, Melanchthon and Pistorius. Granvella remained chairman. The Curia were excluded from direct participation. Yet, they had sent a delegation, and on the request of the Emperor who wanted to soothe Rome, they were accepted as participants. Rome sent Contarini, with the explicit instruction to resist any agreement and to refuse making concessions. Thus the six *collocutors* started their discussions in a tense situation surrounded by representatives of the Estates of the Empire, electors, princes, and delegates of the Curia.[11]

In hindsight we can conclude that the *Regensburg Disputation* was the last meeting between Rome and the Reformation that gave hope for reconciliation and re-unification. Lekkerkerker points to the very serious consequences of the eventual failure of Regensburg for the relationship between Protestants and Roman Catholics 'until today'.[12] Jedin stresses that Regensburg was 'the last serious discussion before the meeting of the Council of Trent to restore ecclesiastical unity and to heal the incurable wound'. Jedin says that this last attempt for re-unification was necessary to pave the way for the Council of Trent and to justify the definite separation that was brought about by Trent.[13]

The participants of Regensburg themselves must also have realised this dimension of finality. There was much at stake for all the involved parties. The Reformation was in full momentum. It was still the main option for the whole of Germany and for other large parts of Europe. Through a religious agreement at the level of the Empire Bucer and his friends tried to pave the way for full victory of the Reformation in the whole Empire and beyond. Later the

---

[11] The prelude to and the course of the religious disputation in Regensburg has been described by various authors, e.g.: C. Augustijn, *De godsdienstgesprekken tussen Rooms-Katholieken en Protestanten van 1538 tot 1541*, Haarlem: De Erven Bohm, 1967; R. Stupperich, *Der Humanismus und die Wiedervereiniging der Religionen*, Leipzig: Heinsius, 1936, chapters 3 and 4; A. Blatter, *Thätigkeit Melanchthons bei den Unionsversuchen 1539-1541*, pp. 9-138; Hollerbach, *Das Religionsgespräch*, chapter 7; Lortz, *Die Reformation*, pp. 211-238.
[12] A.F.N. Lekkerkerker, 'Rechtvaardiging', in: *Protestantse Verkenningen na Vaticanum II*, Den Haag: Boekencentrum, 1967, p. 46.
[13] Jedin, *Kardinal Contarini*, pp.15-17.

Reformer of Strasbourg would experience in the failure of Regensburg a personal defeat and a defeat for the progress of the Reformation. The most important question for the Emperor was whether unity in Germany could be restored under the Habsburg rulers, so that peace and safety in the Empire would be guaranteed. The objectives of the Emperor and the Protestants differed greatly, yet at this point their policies concurred. After the failure of the Regensburg Disputations the Emperor changed his policy and resorted to the use of violence. But he would not be able to maintain permanent unity of the Empire. The Pope and the Curia were in a state of confusion. Would Regensburg be to the advantage of Rome or to its disadvantage? They did not know. That is why Rome's policy for Regensburg was to slow down and win time. In the end Contarini adopted this negative approach of his superiors, although he showed himself very flexible and open to the basic motives of the Protestants. Exactly he was the one who contributed much to the stalemate in the discussions. Rome did not appreciate Contarini's contribution to the discussions. One year after Regensburg, in 1542, he died as a maligned person. After the failure of Regensburg, Gropper distanced himself from the conciliatory 'middle party', and became a champion of the Counter Reformation. Especially those representatives of Rome who were nearest to their Protestant partners, later realised most the impossibility of an agreement between the demands of the Vatican and the vision of the Reformation.

Finally, as we have seen, the Regensburg Disputations were characterised by the movement of Erasmian Religious Humanism. This movement was ready to compromise. In Regensburg it reached its summit and at the same time it found its demise. In Regensburg the 'middle party' disappeared. Consequently the preachers of a humanistically coloured religious tolerance lost their influence. Religious Humanism was unable to give satisfying answers to the questions of theology and politics, neither for Rome nor for the Reformation.

Chapter 2

The Extremes Meet

a. Four Aspects

Now we will discuss some characteristics of the above mentioned documents from the history of the religious disputations in the 1530s and in the early 1540s. We will see that these theological writings aim at bridging the gap between the positions of Rome and of the Reformation. They refer to four aspects of theology, and try to get to a consensus in these fields: (a) the teaching on *Grace*, especially with regard to original sin and justification, (b) the *Ecclesiology*, (c) the teaching on the *Sacraments*, and (d) the teaching on a number of *Practical Issues*.

b. Contarini about the *Confessio Augustana*

The Venetian 'lay' theologian Gasparo Contarini belonged to the very few loyal Roman Catholic theologians in the 16th century who wanted to understand the religious motives of the Reformation from within. Contarini was not a stranger to Luther's understanding of justification. Contarini like Luther believed in justification by faith alone. Jedin comments on Contarini's account of his own conversion. He points to a conspicuous parallel between this description and Luther's discovery when reading *Rom.* 1: 17. Both came to see that God's righteousness is not a demanding or threatening righteousness but a righteousness that is given to those who believe in Christ. In 1511, after a tantalising inward crisis, Contarini became convinced that penance and promises cannot put a tormented soul to rest. Rest and peace is only received by trusting the act of salvation by Christ, who has done enough to reconcile all sins. 'Nobody can justify himself by his own works; one has to take refuge to the grace of God and this grace can only be received by faith in Christ'.[14]

---

[14] Jedin, *Kardinal Contarini*, pp. 9, 10.

As we noted, Contarini had also been present during the Disputation at the Diet of Augsburg in 1530. This Disputation inspired Contarini to make his stand vis-à-vis the confession formulated by Melanchthon. Contarini's *Confutation* was not characterised by highly developed theological learning, but by godly simplicity and practical insight. Here we give a summary of the contents, which runs in accordance to the division in four parts mentioned before.

Teaching on grace. In this important aspect Contarini at the start was in agreement with the intention of the Lutherans. He would agree to their understanding of original sin, if only their view could be somewhat 'improved' and 'interpreted correctly'. Contarini admitted that the Fall of Adam also robbed Adam's descendants of grace, thus they lost the ability of doing good works. However, he rejected the Lutheran position that original sin was an act worked by us, and that after baptism we continue to have original sin.[15]

With regard to *justification* Contarini discerned two aspects, the *imputative* aspect, and the *inherent* aspect. In his *Confutatio* he did not yet work out these aspects as much as later in Regensburg, but the beginnings of this 'duplicity', which he probably derived from Augustine's exegesis of Paul,[16] are undoubtedly there. In his thought the justification of a Christian is participating in God's righteousness. In his natural state man does not have this righteousness. That is why man needs to be born again. We cannot earn justification by our preceding good works, because those works are depraved as a consequence of sin. Man is justified by imputation (*imputatio*) of the grace of Christ, in faith.[17] Faith produces good works. These good works that are a consequence of justification, are to be discerned from the good works that precede faith. The preceding good works do not earn eternal life. However, this is different from the good works that follow. The good works that follow faith still have no earning power in as far as they are expressions of the human soul. However, they are also to be considered as earning eternal life, in as far as they are works of grace that are expressions of the divine principle that is poured out into the reborn soul. Then they are expressions of 'indwelling' or inherent righteousness of the believer. In that sense good works are rewarding and have

---

[15] Jedin, *Kardinal Contarini*, pp. 25, 26.
[16] Cf. F.W. Kantzenbach, *Das Ringen um die Einheit der Kirche im Jahrhundert der Reformation: Vertreter, Quellen und Motive des 'ökumenischen' Gedankens von Erasmus von Rotterdam bis Georg Calixt*, Stuttgart: Evangelischer Verlagswerk, 1957, p. 168.
[17] Jedin, *Kardinal Contarini*, pp. 19-21; Kantzenbach, *Das Ringen*, pp. 142-175.

an earning effect.[18]

It is true that Contarini in his teaching of 'double justification' put more emphasis on the imputed righteousness by God's grace than on the indwelling righteousness of the good works.[19] Yet, his vision of the abilities of (reborn) man was more optimistic than Luther's. This is understandable when we look at Contarini's opinion about the human will. He agreed with Luther that our will cannot do anything good without the grace of God, and that we have to resort to that grace. But he rejected Luther's insight that by nature our will is slavishly bound to sin. Contarini was of the opinion that our will is free, before and after justification. The will of those who do not refuse the impulse of divine grace, will be elevated to a higher level.[20]

In Contarini's teaching on grace there was almost no connection between justification and the sacraments. Moreover, he emphatically stressed sin and faith. These elements in his vision made it possible for him to have discussions with the Lutherans. However, at the same time the possibility of fruitful discussions with the Lutherans was diminished by his description of the good works and of the human will. Contarini's thoughts lacked a systematic approach. They were open for change, which would appear in a later stage.

King Francis I of France (1494-1547) was interested in the Disputations that could lead to reconciliation between the religious parties, because of his humanist orientation and his political interest.

Ecclesiology. With regard to ecclesiological matters Contarini showed much restraint. He was of the opinion that the order in the Church requires a hierarchy of Pope and Bishops. However, he did not define the extent to which the hierarchy has power and authority. Mediating theologians on both sides for the time being preferred to keep the sensitive issue of papal and episcopal power in the background. On the Roman Catholic side there was no consensus on this matter. Sharply defined statements from the Protestant side embarrassed the Roman Catholic party and blocked the discussion with the Lutherans even

---

[18] Jedin, *Kardinal Contarini*, pp. 22-24.
[19] Kanzenbach, *Das Ringen*, pp. 142-175.
[20] Jedin, *Kardinal Contarini*, pp. 26-31.

before it would start.[21] Already before his nomination as a Cardinal in 1535, Contarini became more outspoken about the position of the Pope. In his writing *De Potestate Pontificis* he dared to ascribe to the Pope infallibility in matters of doctrine. However, later he was prepared to make concessions regarding this issue.[22]

Ulrich Zwingli (1484-1531), Reformer at Zürich in Switzerland. He disagreed to Luther concerning the teaching on the Lord's Supper. Bucer's attempts for reconciliation of Zwingli and Luther in Marburg 1529, were a prelude to his work for reconciliation in a wider perspective.

Teaching on the sacraments. Concerning this issue too, Contarini remained rather vague. He critisised Luther's downgrading of auricular confession,[23] and his denouncing of the celibacy,[24] and of mass as a sacrifice.[25] He carefully avoided the term *transubstantiation*, although in a later stage he would tenaciously hold to that word. Yet the contents of the term he defended all the way through. Contarini said that *mass* is a sacrifice and that it was the same sacrifice as on Golgotha, although he admitted that there is a difference, because the manner of sacrificing is new.

Practical issues. Concerning many ecclesiastical institutions and traditions Contarini largely agreed with the Lutherans that they needed reform. He mentioned the following: misuse and idolatry in the veneration of saints,[26] increase in the number and places of mass celebration,[27] activities by ignorant and wrong priests,[28] idolatrous and legalistic use of the rules for fasting.[29]

Contarini was convinced that the Lutherans could be won back if abuses were removed, and if ecclesiastical leaders would stop being egotistic.

---

[21] Jedin, *Kardinal Contarini*, pp. 45, 46.
[22] Kantzenback, *Das Ringen*, p. 167; Jedin, *Kardinal Contarini*, p. 15. In the beginning of the discussions in Regensburg Contarini showed flexibility with regard to the question of the primacy of the Pope. He put the issue at the end of the conference agenda, in order to prevent problems in an early stage.
[23] Jedin, *Kardinal Contarini*, pp. 31-33.
[24] Jedin, *Kardinal Contarini*, pp. 37-40.
[25] Jedin, *Kardinal Contarini*, pp. 40-42.
[26] Jedin, *Kardinal Contarini*, pp.35,36.
[27] Jedin, *Kardinal Contarini*, p.45.
[28] Jedin, *Kardinal Contarini*, p.42.
[29] Jedin, *Kardinal Contarini*, pp. 43,44.

He was of the opinion that 'the errors of the Lutherans' should not be answered by books and refined arguments, but by a 'spotless and humble life, of which the only aim is seeking Christ and the wellbeing of our neighbours'. In all this Contarini was undoubtedly loyal to Rome. He concluded his writing with the solemn promise that he would always 'submit himself to the authority of the Church of Rome ... and obey it without hesitation'.[30] Five years later the Pope made him a Cardinal. Now Contarini was ready to play a significant role in the most important religious Disputation of the 16th century.

c. Gropper's *Enchiridion*

Johannes Gropper was more a systematic theologian than Contarini.[31] He was a humanistically-oriented scholar who was fully involved in the current developments in Germany. As reform-minded adviser to the Archbishop of Cologne, Hermann von Wied, he was present at the Diet of Augsburg in 1530. He was deeply impressed by the religious debates there. Gropper was also moved by the struggle between Luther and Erasmus on the question of the will.[32] Trying to find answers in Roman Catholic tradition, he turned to the Bible and to the Church Fathers. In these years he developed from a relativising Humanist to a Roman Catholic theologian who was ready to take up the challenges of the Lutherans, with the intention of keeping unity under Rome. In 1538 this process of change in his mind had reached completion. Now Roman Catholic tradition determined his thinking. He was convinced that without the Church of Rome there would be no salvation and no Christ.[33] In 1538 Gropper's *Enchiridion* was published, a dogmatic writing that discusses Luther's theology, without mentioning his name though. He tried to answer the questions put forward by the Reformation, without attacking the theological structure of Rome. Here is a summary of Gropper's thought on the four topics mentioned earlier.

Teaching on grace. In Gropper's teaching on grace, similar to that of Contarini, there are two aspects that are possibly conflicting. First, he made a concession to Luther by taking depravity very seriously, as a consequence of

---

[30] Jedin, *Kardinal Contarini*, p.49.
[31] See Kantzenbach, *Das Ringen*, p.168.
[32] Kantzenbach, *Das Ringen*, p. 170.
[33] Kantzenbach, *Das Ringen*, p. 171.

original sin. A heavy stress on the Fall of Man was a common characteristic of conciliatory Roman Catholic theologians in that time. Our original nature is completely depraved, and therefore we deserve eternal death. At the same time, opposing Luther, Gropper stated more emphatically than Contarini the Thomist *analogia-entis-thought* that the Fall of Man has not essentially disturbed the image of God in man. Man still has a free will; he is still able to long for God.[34]

More clearly than Contarini did, Gropper discerned a phase of preparation leading to justification. More than in Contarini's thought he looked upon justification as a process. In describing this, he continued his double approach. On the one hand man is able through a free decision of the will to lift himself up to God. On the other hand, in the preparatory phase, there is the work of the preceding grace (*gratia praeveniens*), that enlarges the abilities of the will. By that preceding grace God equips the will in such a way that man is able to consent freely to justifying grace or to reject it freely. In this thought man himself takes the initiative of starting on the road to justification. In Luther's theology justification results from the sovereign predestination by God. Man is justified because of God's initiative and not because of man's initiative. Gropper's approach was fundamentally different. Preceding grace elevates man, which empowers him to continue, and finally receive the justifying sacrament. Gropper admits that on his way to justification man depends on grace. But when God grants grace, He always looks at the latest moment of initiative of man. Without the consent of the will of man, which results in good initiative, justification cannot be complete. God helps man in getting to these completing initiatives. That is why after the preparatory phase of the *preceding grace* God gives cooperating grace (*gratia cooperans*). In the light of cooperating grace man sees his sinfulness which leads him to repentance, penance and faith.

In this thought man gradually approaches the real act of justification. The dual righteousness (*iustitia duplex*) that we saw in Contarini's description, is even more apparent in Gropper's views. It seems that Gropper discerned three aspects. He recognised that justification is the fruit of faith, it is a gift from God. At the same time it is an activity, a decision by man. Corresponding to this duality in faith there is also a duality in justification, which consequently also has three aspects.

The *first aspect* is Gropper's recognition that justification results from

---

[34] Lipgen, *Johannes Gropper*, pp. 81-84, 105, where he says that man is able to 'Regungen der Sensucht nach Gott' (movements of passion for God).

imputation (*imputatio*). The guilt of sin attributed to us, and the resulting sentence of death, are removed because of what Christ has earned on Golgotha through His sacrifice. Christ's righteousness is imputed to us. Lipgen says that this imputative element in Gropper's thought is an addition to the Thomist teaching, which he derived from Augustine, even deviating from the Church Father in a way. Gropper also was vague with respect to the relationship between justification and the sacraments. We noticed a similar vagueness in Contarini's descriptions. According to Lipgen, Gropper believed that the act of justification is connected to the sacraments, but he did not clearly say so.[35] We will see that Gropper was not vague in his ecclesiology, which was clearly determined by the sacraments.

The *second aspect* of justification in Gropper's description was in line with Thomas. Justification is not only a matter of divine imputation, but also a matter of man himself. Justification is not only *imputative* by God, but also *effective* in man. There is *imputative* righteousness, but there is also *inherent* righteousness. The inherent righteousness leads to good works. By doing good works, man confirms that he is justified. And the outcome of judgment on entering eternal life depends on these good works. It seems that Gropper, although he stressed *imputative righteouness*, eventually remained in agreement with the Thomist teaching that was recognised by Rome. In Thomist teaching justification is the result of a process of cooperation between the work of God and the work of man. Exactly this idea was rejected by the Reformation. Gropper could never have been a serious candidate for religious Disputations with the Lutherans, if his teachings had not comprised more than this.

Gropper gives an important addition to his idea of inherent righteousness or effective justification. We may call this the *third aspect* of Gropper's teaching on justification. The life of works of a justified person is not sufficient for reaching to the required state of holiness. Good works cannot sanctify a person, they cannot make him holy. This is because of the remaining effect of sin in the life of a believer. There is still the coveting (*concupiscientia*), the greed, the cupidity in the life of Christians. Luther had also stressed this. The new creature struggles against this, while trying to progress in renewal and purity, but the result is insufficient. Our inherent righteousness can only be complete, or perfect, because it is the work of God. But our own works are not perfect. They are not complete. The cooperation

---

[35] Lipgen, *Johannes Gropper*, pp. 82-95, 105; See also Kantzenbach, *Das Ringen*, p.171, who opposes Stupperich's view that Gropper derived his teaching of double justification directly from Erasmus.

needed in acquiring salvation, in Gropper's opinion, has to be perfect. From the angle of man there is an insurmountable obstacle here. Therefore at this point Gropper has to go back to the *imputed righteousness* of Christ. In addition to the inherent righteousness, man has to turn to an *external power* that can add to this righteousness so that his works become perfect. This extra righteousness is found in the *imputative righteousness* of Christ. The perfect work of Christ is added to our incomplete works. Although our good works are required for the realisation of justification, we can only exist before God 'as far as we have been in communication with the righteousness of Christ'.[36]

Gropper was urged to this significant addition because he knew that sin remains powerful in the life of believers. Here we see a parallel with Luther's emphasis on the remaining power of sin. But Gropper's conception of double or rather triple justification was considered by Luther as a compromise and therefore an unfit tool for unity. Irreconcilable matters were joined together. According to the Reformer of Wittenberg, this could not be a durable basis for an agreement.[37]

Lipgen says that Gropper's view belongs to a tradition of learning that in Rome, previous to the Council of Trent, was still recognised as Roman Catholic. Gropper embraced the Church of Rome, but he realised that the current teachings on justification were justifiably criticised. That is why he wanted to make corrections. He rejected the radical stance of Luther, but he recognised that Luther took things seriously. As long as his thought was still developing, he met with sympathy of conciliatory representatives of the Reformation. But in a later stage, influenced by the Council of Trent, he would adapt to the line of the *Counter Reformation*. The beginning of this turn we already see in the end of his *Enchiridion*: 'Everything in this book we submit to the judgment of the Holy See which we rightfully honour'.[38]

Ecclesiology. In his teaching on grace Gropper to some extent was open to the Protestants. This is less so in his views of the Church and the Sacraments. In his *Enchiridion* the Bible and Tradition are practically equivalent. Both rest on the Church which has the power to teach through Word and Sacraments. The Church is the body of Christ that continues to live, and the Holy Spirit directs its decisions. The Church has to denounce heretics and schismatics because they damage the bond of love. Outside the Sacraments of

---

[36] Lipgen, *Johannes Gropper*, pp. 100-108.
[37] Kantzenbach, *Das Ringen*, p. 174.
[38] Lipgen, *Johannes Gropper*, p. 111.

the Church there is no salvation.

Especially in his description of the mass Gropper shows that he looked upon the Church as a sacramental institution of salvation. In it the sacrifice of Christ is continuing. Christ's sacrifice through the Church is re-enacted daily as a source of life. Only those who participate in this act of the Church, are in community with the Christ. Gropper also recognised the hierarchy of priests and the papacy. All priests have similar spiritual authority, but the successor of Peter is to edify the Church and to safeguard its teaching.[39]

Practical issues. Gropper was in favour of Reform. This was most apparent in his diligent attempts to remove practical abuses. The Reform Decretals issued by the Council of the Archbishopric of Cologne in 1536 were written by him. These decretals tried to create order in the nomination and the functioning of priests. They emphasised the necessity of pastoral care, the administering of the Word, and the removing of abuses in the administration of the Sacraments.[40]

d. Bucer and the *Leipzig Draft for Re-union*

Only recently historians have realised the significance of Bucer as a champion of the unity of the Church. Bucer realised deeply that unity belongs to the constituting characteristics of the Church. Bucer worked hard for unity of the Church of Jesus Christ.

First he tried to keep unity in the Reformation movement. That is why he organised a meeting between Luther and Zwingli, which eventually took place in Marburg in 1529. He felt pity when Luther adamantly refused to agree with Zwingli on an aspect of the teaching on the Lord's Supper.

Secondly, Bucer attempted to get to an agreement with followers of the Radical Reformation, especially with the Anabaptists. He accepted their challenge that Christians should lead holy lives, and he adapted his idea of church organisation to the principle that the church is the communion of saints.[41] That is why Bucer strongly emphasised that the Christian congregation is the communion of people that are set apart to grow in sanctification. One year before the meeting in Leipzig on re-union he published *On true Pastoral*

---

[39] Lipgen, *Johannes Gropper*, pp. 67-78; Kantzenbach, *Das Ringen*, pp. 170-175.

[40] Lipgen, *Johannes Gropper*, pp. 55-63.

[41] S. Paas, *From Galilee to the Atlantic: A History of the Church in the West*, Zomba: Kachere, 2004, pp. 194ff.

Care (1538), in which he worked out and harmoniously combined his teaching on the Church and his teaching on pastoral theology.[42]

Thirdly, considering the teaching and the practice in the Early Church, Bucer thought it possible to achieve reconciliation with the Roman Catholics. They only would have to agree to the free proclamation of the Gospel. The servants of the Church should not rule like kings, they should graze the sheep in the pastures of the Word. This free functioning of faithful preaching of the Word will start a process that makes errors and abuses disappear. If the other party would only accept this principle, Bucer would be prepared to make concessions to them. Bucer was even prepared to tolerate the Pope. In a writing of 1534 dedicated to the French King Francis I, Bucer stated that he did not aim at the destruction of the Papacy, if only the Pope and the Bishops would open the Scriptures and would use their power to edify the Church, not to destroy it.[43] Because of his involvement in the writing of the *Leipzig Draft* (1539), he was made a participant to the religious Disputation in Regensburg. Now we will summarise and discuss this document, which will be indicated as *LD*.[44]

Teaching on grace. In its teaching on grace the LD undoubtedly tended to be Lutheran. Original sin has so utterly depraved natural man that man cannot do good and is judged by God's anger. However, in His mercy, through Word and Spirit, God grants to man the faith so completely 'that Jesus wants to forgive all his sins and give him eternal life; then man through this faith without the help of the works that he did preceding grace, is made righteous before God, a child of God and an heir of eternal salvation'.[45] Unlike Gropper's *Enchiridion* the *LD* did not indicate a human moment of initiative as a condition of divine grace. *LD* did use the term *free will* of man, 'either from the flesh to do evil, or from grace to do good'.[46] Here we see not only the influence of Luther, but also the influence of Erasmus. However this free-will-passage is limited, because its context emphasises total depravity as a consequence of the Fall of man and the sovereignty of God's grace. The main emphasis is on *imputative justification*.

---

[42] M. Bucer, *Von der wahren Seelsorge*, Strasbourg, 1538. See also: W. van 't Spijker, *The Ecclesiastical Offices in the Thought of Martin Bucer* (translated by John Vriend and Lyle D. Bierma), Leyden: Brill, 1996. See also: W. van 't Spijker, 'Straatsburg', in: W. Balke e.a., *Luther en het gereformeerde protestantisme*, Den Haag: Boekencentrum, 1982, chapter 2.
[43] Cf. Kantzenbach, *Das Ringen*, pp. 90,91,124.
[44] Cardauns, *Zur Geschichte*, pp. 85-108.
[45] Cardauns, *Zur Geschichte*, pp. 86 (*LD* Article 1).
[46] Cardauns, *Zur Geschichte*, pp. 87,88 (*LD* Article 2).

Yet, Cardauns is of the opinion that in the *LD*, Bucer and his friends abandoned the Protestant (i.e. imputative) thought of justification. He points to the position of good works in the *LD*, and thinks that good works in the *LD* earn salvation.[47] It is true that in the *LD* there is a strong connection between good works and salvation, in the sense that the necessity of good works is stressed. But not for one moment the Protestant line of thought is lost sight of, because it is carefully avoided to give the good works any earning quality. It is said that a believer lives in Christ and that Christ lives in him and that necessarily the result of this is the doing of good works. 'Because the Lord wants to judge all people in accordance with their works, good works in true faith and love are necessary for salvation and the Lord rewards temporarily and eternally because of the good works. However, he does not reward them because of the value of these works in themselves, but because of grace and through the merit of Christ, who works out these works in His people and thus crowns His gifts in them'. These words sound Bucerian. They emphasise that sanctification is a necessity and a matter of course. But the centrality of Christ's merit in justification also applies to sanctification. In Christ believers are made righteous and in Christ they are made holy. The necessity of good works is not diminished when the *LD* says that 'they are still imperfect', and that 'continually we have to pray for forgiveness and grace', and that always 'we have to seek true comfort and assurance of conscience in Christ'.[48] These words are in agreement with the Wittenberg Reformation, but even more clearly with the Strasbourg and the Geneva Reformation. Good works are not the foundation of salvation, yet they are necessary.

At this point there is a conspicuous difference with Gropper's *Enchiridion*. Although there were imputative moments in Gropper's description, he looked upon justification as a continuing process of collaboration between divine and human activity. Here Gropper and the *LD* basically disagree. In the *LD* the human component, expressed in good works, is necessary, but justification is fully the result of Christ's merit. Both, God's justifying judgment and the effective sanctification of life, are imputed. This explains why Gropper's thought that good works are imputatively completed by Christ's righteousness, did not occur in the *LD*. Gropper's description implies that good works, at least partly, can possess man's own righteousness. In the *LD* all good works are fully the imputative work of Christ in man who believes

---

[47] Cardauns, *Zur Geschichte*, p. 10.
[48] Cardauns, *Zur Geschichte*, pp. 86, 87 (*LD*, Article 1).

in the forgiveness of sins and the promise of eternal life, which work is applied by God's Spirit.

Ecclesiology. The *LD* criticises sharply the abuses that were condoned or even committed by the hierarchy of Rome. The document remains vague on the character of the Church as such. But the task of the Church is described in clear words: preaching the Word of God and administering the Sacraments.[49] The Church has to punish public sins and exclude persistent sinners from the Sacraments.[50] The position of the special servants of the Church is widely discussed in the *LD*. They are ordained by the laying on of hands. The *LD* does not discuss the idea of Rome that ordination is a Sacrament. Celibacy and monastic vows are rejected.[51] The *LD* thinks in terms of continuation of the ecclesiastical hierarchy, but wants to limit its power. Nobility, citizens and the people together choose their pastors and bishops. Except for their ecclesiastical responsibilities, members of the clergy are submitted to civil authority.[52] The *LD* leaves space for the Pope, but only as a universal pastor and overseer, and it is of the opinion that many Popes have led the people away from Christ.[53]

Sacraments. In the *LD* the Sacraments are dealt with in connection with the teaching on the Church. Yet, the Church is not looked upon as a Sacrament. The character of the Sacraments in the framework of the teaching on grace does not get much attention either. The *LD* does not oppose the number of seven Sacraments as maintained by Rome. In the way of administering the Sacraments many abuses are detected. The eucharist is explained in a Lutheran sense, although the question of a change of the substance of the elements is avoided. Communion with only bread is rejected in the *LD*, and it advises against mass without communicants.[54] Other recommendations and demands are: the necessity of repentance and penance at auricular confession,[55] allowing the optional character of confirmation and extreme unction,[56] the need for

---

[49] Cardauns, *Zur Geschichte*, p. 86 (*LD*, Article 1).
[50] Cardauns, *Zur Geschichte*, pp. 88-90 (*LD*, Article 3).
[51] Cardauns, *Zur Geschichte*, pp.104,105 (*LD*, Article 11).
[52] Cardauns, *Zur Geschichte*, pp. 106-108 (*LD*, Article 15).
[53] Cardauns, *Zur Geschichte*, pp. 97-102 (*LD,* Article 7). 'so seindt auch in vilen jaren wenig bepst gewesen, die wir nicht haben als der enthchrist meyden und fliehen sollen, bey verlust der gnaden Gottes und des ewigen lebens' (in may years there have been few popes whom we should not have shun and fled from as anti-Christ, because of the danger of losing the grace of God and eternal life)
[54] Cardauns, *Zur Geschichte*, pp. 91-96 (*LD*, Article 5).
[55] Cardauns, *Zur Geschichte*, pp. 88-90 (*LD*, Article 3).
[56] Cardauns, *Zur Geschichte*, pp. 96, 97 (*LD*, Article 6), pp. 102, 103 (*LD*, Article 8).

creating order (by the civil authorities!) in the rules for fasting,[57] stopping exorcist activities at baptism,[58] the abolition of the veneration of saints.[59]

---

[57] Cardauns, *Zur Geschichte*, pp. 103, 104 (*LD*, Articles 9 and 10).
[58] Cardauns, *Zur Geschichte*, p. 90 (*LD*, Article 4).
[59] Cardauns, *Zur Geschichte*, pp. 105, 106 (*LD*, Article 12).

Chapter 3

Rapprochement and Separation

a. Regensburg 1541

The secret discussions between Gropper and Bucer in Hagenau and Worms (1540/ 1541) produced a document that at the Diet of Regensburg would be the starting point for religious diplomacy at high level. In Latin this book is entitled

View of the city of Regensburg (Latin: Ratisbona) where in 1541, at the initiative of Habsburg Emperor Charles V, the Disputation between Roman Catholic and Protestant theologians took place. The city is located in Bavaria, South-East Germany, at the confluence of the rivers Danube and Regen.

Liber Ratisbonensis, i.e. the *Regensburg Book* (*RB*). In the previous chapter we discussed Gropper's *Enchiridion* and the *Leipzig Draft of Re-union* (*LD*) that determined the direction of the Regensburg Disputations, or at least considerably influenced the contents of the *RB*. The *RB* is more in agreement to Gropper's *Enchiridion* than to the *LD*. That is why generally Gropper is supposed to be the editor of the *RB* draft. The contents are closer to the Roman Catholic position than to the Protestant stance.[60] Prior to the discussion of the

---

[60] Cf. Cardauns, *Zur Geschichte*, pp. 19-23.

RB draft, as to some twenty issues, Contarini sharpened its contents in favour of Roman Catholicism. Yet, it would become apparent soon that the strict ones in the Roman Catholic party could not stomach many passages in the document.

The disputations in Regensburg lasted from 27th April to 12th July 1541. For a full account we refer to some excellent books on the subject.[61] In this study we summarise the main aspects, arranging them according to the fourfold division applied before. To each aspect we first will describe the contents of the *RB* draft that were presented to the participants, and then we'll look in more detail at the discussions on the draft text.

b. Teaching on Grace

The first five Articles deal with the teaching on grace. Concerning the cause and the consequences of original sin, *RB* is not really deviating from *Enchiridion* and *LD*. This is also true for the will of man. The will is considered to be free in all the three documents. The issue of justification is described in Article five. The title of this article in the *RB* draft already indicates an important difference with the *LD* and to a lesser degree with *Enchiridion*: 'On the Rebirth and Justification of Man through Grace and Merit, through Faith and Works'. Man is justified in a two-fold manner. On the one hand man is justified through faith, without preceding good works. On the other hand he is justified through the good works that are produced by faith. Faith in Christ is not sufficient if not the progress of good works is connected to it. In this way the good works in the *RB* draft are more or less loosened from faith itself, whereas they are made a necessary extra foundation for the *receiving* of justifying faith. Cooperation between grace and good works is in the forefront. The thought, in the *LD*, that justification is solely produced by the imputed merit of Christ, is pushed back here. And also Gropper's 'third aspect', of *imputative* addition to the good works from Christ's righteousness, cannot be found in the *RB* draft.[62]

What was the result of the discussions on this matter? The surprising thing of Regensburg 1541 is that within a week the collocutors agreed on the

---

[61] C. Augustijn, *De godsdienstgesprekken tussen Rooms-Katholieken en Protestanten van 1538 tot 1541*, Haarlem: De Erven Bohm, 1967; R. Stupperich, *Der Humanismus und die Wiedervereiniging der Religionen*, Leipzig: Heinsius, 1936, chapters 3 and 4; A. Blatter, *Thätigkeit Melanchthons bei den Unionsversuchen 1539-1541*, pp. 9-138; Hollerbach, *Das Religionsgespräch*, chapter 7; Lortz, *Die Reformation*, pp. 211-238.
[62] Blatter, *Thätigkeit Melanchthons*, pp.78, 79; Lipgen, *Johannes Gropper*, pp. 127, 128.

nucleus of the teaching on grace. They put aside the draft text of Article five, because it sounded too Roman Catholic in Protestant ears, and also Gropper et. al. could not agree to it. The collocutors also rejected proposals by Eck, Contarini[63] and Melanchthon.[64] Then, mainly by Gropper's contribution, a text was drafted to which all participants apparently agreed. The text of the new article looks like Gropper's description of justification in the *Enchiridion*. It also comprises elements that remind of the *LD*. It is a formula of compromise, that carefully avoids attacking the stances of the Roman Catholic Curia and of Luther. The Roman Catholic party seems to have made the biggest concession.

Just like the *Enchiridion* the new Article five of the *RB* draft says that the pardoned sinner receives double righteousness, i.e. *imputed* righteousness and *inherent* righteousness. Man is justified by the living faith that embraces the imputed righteousness of Christ. This imputation is 'the essential cause' of justification. Both Gropper and Contarini admitted that man's merit man can play no role here. Participants offered no opinion on the question whether there is a causative connection between the Sacraments and the imputation of righteousness. The *Enchiridion* had not commented on this either. Then the article says that justification is through faith in the forgiveness of sins and the promise of eternal life, and that this faith is effective through love. Through love faith operates in man and creates inward (*inherent*) righteousness. This righteousness is a gift from God. In love it expresses itself, in repentance, in the fear of God and in good works. The Article emphatically states that man cannot trust this inward righteousness as if it were his justification. Only the imputed righteousness of Christ is the foundation of trusting faith. The desire for sin (*concupiscientia*) remains and our works are not perfect. Yet the Article says that there is some causative connection between good works and justification. Good works are 'the formal cause' of our justification.[65]

The new Article five of the *RB* draft offered to conciliatory participants the possibility of looking at justification from two different angles. Imputation is 'the essential cause' of justification and good works are 'the formal cause' of justification. The first angle represented more or less the Lutheran stance, and in the second angle one could recognise a weakened form of the Roman Catholic stance. Although the Protestant contribution seems to be dominant, the

---

[63] Contarini's *Epistola de Iustificatione*, just like Gropper's *Enchiridion* defended a 'double justification', but more than Gropper, Contarini emphasised the *imputatio*. Cf. Kantzenbach, *Das Ringen*, p. 167.
[64] Blatter, *Thätigkeit Melanchthons*, pp. 79,80.
[65] Blatter, *Thätigkeit Melanchthons*, p.83; Lipgen, *Johannes Gropper*, pp. 128,129; Augustijn, *De godsdienstgesprekken*, chapters 7 and 8.

article is (consciously?) formulated in such a way that two interpretations are possible. The options of interpretation are answers to the question of the effect of faith. In the Protestant view faith effectuates the justifying act of the sovereign God. In the Roman Catholic view faith effectuates the process of justification in which there is cooperation between the good works of the free human will and the grace of God.

This agreement at Regensburg was not given a long life. After a brief period of joy for the participants and their friends the new Article five was flooded by criticism from both sides of the religious divide.

Let us first look at comments by contemporary mouthpieces of the two parties. Rome was not happy with the agreed text that had been sent to the Curia by an elated Contarini. Soon the Cardinal-legate was reproached of Lutheran heresy, and he was officially admonished to behave more strictly. Pope Paul III was of the opinion that the formula included Protestant elements, or at least elements that they could be interpreted in a Protestant way, and therefore the new article was not acceptable. Luther too rejected the Article. In his view the text was diffuse and characterised by half-heartedness. He wanted to keep to the clear teaching of justification by faith alone. Yet Luther did not reject the Article unconditionally. He only instructed Melanchthon not to accept it if there would be no agreement on the other issues of the Regensburg Disputation.⁶⁶

Johann Eck (1486-1543), German theologian, who publicly opposed Martin Luther in a Disputation at Leipzig (1519), and contributed much to counteract Protestantism, i.e. as a participant of the Disputation in Regensburg on the Roman Catholic side.

Bucer was of the opinion that the wording of the Article left much to be desired. Yet, he thought that the agreement was a victory for the Protestant party. Even John Calvin († 1564), his fellow worker at Strasbourg, who was present in Regensburg as an observer, considered the result as moderately positive. He wrote to Guillaume Farel:

> 'Finally a text was formulated that, after some improvements from both sides, was accepted. I know that the many concessions of the opponents will amaze you ... Because our people are maintaining mainly the true teaching, so that

---

⁶⁶ Blatter, *Thätigkeit Melanchthons*, pp. 83-85, including Luther's words in defence of his teaching on justification: 'Dabei bleiben wir, die ist kurz und klar; dawider mag sturmen Teufel, Eck un Heinz'; See also: Augustijn, *De godsdienstgesprekken*, chapter 8a.

the formula contains nothing which is not in our writings too. I know that you desire a much clearer statement and in this you have an ally. Yet, considering the kind of people we are dealing with, you will realise that much has been attained'.[67]

John Calvin (1509-1564). At the time of the Disputation he lived as a refugee in Strasbourg, where he was influenced by the teachings of Bucer, and agreed to the attempts that were made for restoration of Christian unity.

Let us also listen to some voices of the 20th century. Lipgen summarises the Roman Catholic objections against the new formula of compromise of 1541. He says that that the inclusion of the imputed righteousness takes away the strength of the inherent righteousness. He reproaches Gropper, who in his opinion consciously transgressed the boundary of Roman Catholic dogma. In the *Enchiridion*, imputation only had a bearing on the extreme moment in the final phase of the justification process, when the sinner before God's throne has to admit that his good works are imperfect. This in Lipgen's thought still is legitimate Roman Catholic teaching. But in the new Article of the RB draft the process of justification is enveloped by *imputation*. Justification is no longer a process of cooperation, it has become a one-sided act of God. Lipgen concludes that in this imputation formula the position of the good works has diminished considerably.[68] Lekkerkerker, on the other hand, is of the opinion that the new Article still describes justification as a process in which man's good works play a decisive role.[69] These opposed interpretations illustrate the apparent dualism in the text of the new article.

c. Ecclesiology

The collocutors at Regensburg found many more problems in the Articles on the Church[70] of the *RB* draft, than in the passages of the teaching on grace. Whereas the *LD* consciously kept the formula on the Church vague, the *RB* draft and also the *Enchiridion* defined the Church much more sharply. They

---

[67] Lekkerkerker, 'Rechtvaardiging', in *Protestantse Verkenningen*, p. 45.
[68] Lipgen, *Johannes Gropper*, p. 129.
[69] Lekkerkerker, 'Rechtvaardiging', in *Protestantse Verkenningen*, p. 46.
[70] *RB* Articles 6-8, 11, 19, 22.

tended to describe the Church as a sacramental institution of salvation, although this term was not used. Article 9 condemns all who secede from the Church. In the context of Regensburg this leads the Roman Catholic party to call the Lutherans schismatics. The Church has the highest authority to expound the Bible. Decisions by general Church Councils are infallible. The minority has to accept the decisions of the majority. The *RB* maintained a hierarchical order of the Church, although much stress was put on the *collegiality* of the Bishops. The Church on earth is put under a Head, the Bishop of Rome. This practically identifies the Church with the papal empire. The Primate was instituted by Christ. The *RB* left the question of the celibacy of the clergy open. Disciplinary measures were recommended to combat abuses among priests and other servants of the Church.[71]

On 3rd May the first Articles on Ecclesiology[72] were tabled. After the euphoria about the agreement on Justification the discussion on the Church was a disillusionment. The discussions got stuck on Article 9. The main obstacle appeared to be the stated infallibility of Church Councils. Melanchthon did not see much point in the continuation of the Disputation. He emphatically objected to the idea of ecclesiastical authority above the authority of Holy Scriptures. The Word of God is always higher. That is why Church Councils can err. The real Church is not an institution determined by the hierarchy and the Sacraments, but the Church is the communion of believers who have accepted the Bible to be their highest authority. Bucer agreed to Melanchthon's arguments, yet he wanted to continue the discussions. Nevertheless it was decided to postpone the discussion of this part of the *RB*.[73]

In a later stage they reached some agreement on unity as a characteristic of the Church.[74] Then, on 20th May, the Article on ecclesiastical hierarchy as a distinct subject was on the agenda.[75] The Article was not well received by the Protestants, especially the section on the primacy of the Pope. To them maintaining the Papacy was unacceptable. Melanchthon also turned against the Episcopal system as such. He had no use for a supreme Bishop, and he denied that Bishops have taken the place of the Apostles and that they are

---

[71] Blatter, *Thätigkeit Melanchthons*, pp. 88-90; Cardauns, *Zur Geschichte*, pp. 19-23; Augustijn, *De godsdienstgesprekken*, chapter 6; Lipgen, *Johannes Gropper*, p.130.
[72] *RB*, Articles 6-9.
[73] Blatter, *Thätigkeit Melanchthons*, pp. 89-90; Augustijn, *De godsdienstgesprekken*, chapter 8; Lipgen, *Johannes Gropper*, p.130.
[74] *RB*, Article 18.
[75] *RB*, Article 19.

entitled to institute or change ceremonies beyond the Word of God.

Bucer acted more tolerantly than Melanchthon. He also rejected the Papacy and the practical behaviour of the Episcopal hierarchy. But he hoped that the Roman Catholic system would collapse spontaneously if a religious agreement in Germany leaving out the Curia, would open the way for the free proclamation of the Gospel.[76]

d. Teaching on the Sacraments

In the *RB* draft the teaching on the Sacraments[77] was rather systematically connected to the character of the Church. Here the text clearly differed from the *LD* in which the Sacraments were discussed separately. As to ordination and baptism the *RB* and *LD* did not differ much. Confirmation and extreme unction as Sacraments were rejected by the *LD* and maintained by the *RB*. There was a Roman Catholic tendency in the *RB* passage on the mass.[78] Although the controversial word *transubstantiation* was not mentioned in the draft text, it was stated that after consecration the real body and blood of Christ 'are truly and substantially present' in the elements of bread and wine. Only ordained priests can administer mass. They may administer it in the absence of communicants.[79]

In Regensburg the discussions on the Sacraments took more time than any other topic, from 4th May to 19th May, for eight days they discussed the Article on the mass and the eucharist. Contarini insisted that the word *transubstantiation* be included in the text. To Melanchthon, however, the idea of substantial change of bread and wine, was an expression of idolatry. He would 'rather die' than accept the term and its contents.

Again Bucer tried to prevent a rupture. He discerned within the Roman Catholic party a conciliatory group of those 'who earnestly want the truth'. Like Melanchthon he rejected the idea of transubstantiation and related things like carrying around and praying to the elements of the eucharist. But he did not want to push the opponents away, if only they would allow Reforms in other

---

[76] Blatter, *Thätigkeit Melanchthons*, pp. 114-116; Augustijn, *De godsdienstgesprekken*, chapter 8b; Lipgen, *Johannes Gropper*, p.130.
[77] *RB*, Articles 10-17.
[78] RB, Article 14.
[79] Blatter, *Thätigkeit Melanchthons*, p. 91; Lipgen, *Johannes Gropper*, p.130, Cardauns, *Zur Geschichte*, pp.19-23.

issues. If only the Word of God can run freely, eventually they will voluntarily do away with their errors. By this attitude of tolerance Bucer endangered his position in the Lutheran party who were determined to reject the Roman Catholic idea of the mass.

In the meantime the discussions were dragging on. Some agreement was reached as to the Sacraments in general,[80] ordination,[81] baptism,[82] confirmation,[83] marriage,[84] and extreme unction.[85] Yet a basic contradiction became more and more apparent. It was the contradiction between on the one hand the idea that God given salvation is determined by the Sacraments, and on the other hand the thought that God reveals and communicates his salvation to those who believe the Gospel. In other words, it was the contradiction between salvation as an ecclesiastical gift to the receiver of the Sacraments administered by a priest, and salvation as God's free gift to anyone who believes in Christ. During the discussion on auricular confession[86] this difference came into the open. Gropper was of the opinion that a priest, who was to decide on absolution, had to receive an exact list of the sins committed by the confessant. This indirectly put emphasis on the idea that 'lay people' for their salvation depend on members of the ecclesiastical hierarchy. Salvation is received through the sacramental acts of the administrators of the Sacraments. The Protestant collocutors rejected this thought as undermining the all embracing effect of grace and faith. We conclude that in the discussions on the Sacraments the differences between Rome and the (Lutheran) Reformation were surfacing. A breach seemed unavoidable.

e. Practical Issues

The final Articles of the *RB* draft[87] dealt with a rather large number of practical issues. The text considered favourably the invocation of saints, the usage of statues, the veneration of relics, monastic vows, and disciplinary measures for

---

[80] *RB*, Article 10.
[81] *RB*, Article 11.
[82] *RB*, Article 12.
[83] *RB*, Article 13.
[84] *RB*, Article 17.
[85] *RB*, Article 18.
[86] *RB*, Article 15.
[87] *RB*, Articles 20-23.

clergy and people. As far as they were tabled, these issues were discussed in a climate that was not very conducive anymore for the reaching of agreements. No positive results were achieved. The issue of mass returned to the table briefly, now the practical side of it. The Protestants rejected the absence of communicants, the withholding of the 'lay-cup', and the use of Latin in administering the Sacraments. They also demanded that mass had to be disposed of its current sacrificial character. But there was no positive response. Furthermore, no agreement was reached concerning the proposed disciplinary measures.[88]

---

[88] Blatter, *Thätigkeit Melanchthons*, pp.116, 117; Augustijn, *De godsdienstgesprekken*, chapter 8d.

Chapter 4

Deeper Unity of Dogma

a. Church and Sacraments

In the literature that I consulted there is much agreement on the breaking point in the 16th century religious Disputations between Rome and the Reformation. It seems fair to conclude that the religious Disputation in Regensburg in 1541 miscarried because of diverging opinions on the Church and on the Sacraments. [89] This is remarkable because the participants had attained to a far reaching agreement on a wider issue, the teaching on grace. The parties came close to one another on the original situation of man before the Fall, original sin, the human will, and on justification. On the issue of justification a text was formulated that was accepted by all participants. Although this was very promising, the Disputation failed when the topics of Church and Sacraments were discussed. How could this happen?

Varying answers have been given to the question of what caused the failure of Regensburg 1541. Often certain persons are being blamed, e.g. the insincerity

Pope Paul III (Alessandro Farnese, 1468-1549), promoted reforms in the Roman Catholic Church, but he turned against the Protestant Reformation, e.g, by approving of the aims of the Jesuits, and restoring the Inquisition. He rejected the final results of the Regensburg Disputation.

---

[89] Lortz, *Die Reformation*, p. 232: 'In den Artikeln, die mit dem katholischen Kirchenbegriff unmittelbahr zusammenhängen, Sakramente, Transubstantion, Priestertum, Kirche, blieb man in schroffen Gegensatz zu einander' (In the articles directly connected to the Catholic understanding of the Church, sacraments, transubstantiation, priesthood, Church, they remained in strong contradiction to one another). Lekkerkerker, 'Rechtvaardiging', in *Protestantse Verkenningen*, p.46, says that a controversy remained concerning Church and Sacraments, 'which was explosive with regard the transubstantiation, the adoration, reservation, and procession' of the elements of the mass. Lipgen, *Johannes Gropper*, p.44, draws the attention to the fact that even before Regensburg at the Diet of Augsburg the sacrificial character of the mass was the bone of contention that made the discussions fail.

of Emperor Charles V, the stubbornness of Luther, the harsh attitude of the Elector of Saxony, the bigamy of the Count of Hessen, the crafty intentions of the Roman Catholic Electors, the inconsistency and stubborn tenacity of Contarini, the irreconcilable fanatism of Eck, the stubbornness of Melanchthon, the laxity of Bucer, the double-heartedness of Gropper, the narrow minded lust for power of the Curia and the Pope, the bigotry and intolerance of many which did not allow space for religious Humanism.

b. Deeper Unity not Appreciated

There may be some truth in all these accusations. But they do not reach to the level where a satisfying answer can be found to the question why representatives of Rome and the Reformation could agree on a statement on justification, whereas they failed to recognise one another with regard to the Church and the sacraments. It seems the cause of this failure in the first place was a lack of appreciation of all the aspects (*loci*) of the Christian teaching. The teaching on grace, ecclesiology and the sacraments are interrelated; they constitute an unbreakable unity. To a great extent, the position taken in one aspect of theology determines the position one takes concerning the other aspects.

The collocutors in Regensburg were pressurised by political and ecclesiastical circumstances and propelled by the spirit of their time. That is why in their eagerness to reach an agreement on justification they did not look well enough at the consequences for the other fields of theology. A joint declaration on justification should have taken into account the wider framework of theology and the necessity of seeing eye to eye in other fields as well. Free grace and sacramental grace each produce their own kind of ecclesiology and Church. The new text of Article five on justification could not reconcile these two ecclesiologies. It was too much a formula of compromise. It failed to grasp the cornerstone of theology. That is why it lacked the strength that could have re-united the torn Christianity of the 16th century in the Church of Christ.

Kachere Series
P.O. Box 1037, Zomba, Malawi
email: kachere@globemw.net
web: www.sdnp.org.mw/Kachereseries

This book is part of the **Kachere Series**, the publications arm of the **Department of Theology and Religious Studies of the University of Malawi**. A range of books on religion, culture and society in or regarding Malawi is published under the categories: Kachere Books, Kachere Monographs, Kachere Texts, Kachere Studies, Kachere Theses, and Mvunguti Books.

James N. Amanze, *African Traditional Religion: The Case of the Bimbi Cult*
D. Bone (ed.), *Malawi's Muslims: A Historical Perspective*
Joseph Booth, *Africa for the Africans* (ed. Laura Perry)
J.W.M. van Breugel, *Chewa Traditional Religion*
Beryl Brough, *Saint Johnson of Lake Malawi*
J.C. Chakanza (ed.), *Collection of Pastoral Letters*
--, *Wisdom of the People*
--, *Voices of Preachers in Protest*
--, *Islam Week in Malawi*
J.C. Chakanza and Kenneth R. Ross, *Religion in Malawi: An Annotated Bibliography*
Felix Chingota, *The Use of the Concept of Fear in the Book of Deuteronomy*
Masauko Chipembere, Robert Rotberg (eds), *Hero of the Nation*
Henry Church, *Theological Education that Makes a Difference: Church Growth in the Free Methodist Church in Malawi and Zimbabwe*
Rijk van Dijk, Ria Reis, Marja Spierenburg (eds), *The Political Aspects of Healing in Southern Africa*
Harry England, *A Democracy of Chameleons*
Klaus Fiedler, *Christianity and African Culture: German Protestant Missionaries in Tanzania*
--, *Joseph Booth in Melbourne*
Klaus Fiedler, Paul Gundani, Hilary Mijoga (eds), *Theology Cooked in an African Pan*
Peter G. Forster, *T. Cullen Young: Missionary and Anthropologist*
Richard Gordon, *Transforming Psalms*
Clara Henderson, *Rolling Away the Stone: The Africanisation of Christian Music by Presbyterian Mvano Women in Southern Malawi*
David Hulme and Marshal Murphree (eds), *African Wildlife & Livelihood: The Promise and Performance of Community Conservation*
Patrick A. Kalilombe, *Doing Theology at Grassroots: Theological Essays from Malawi*
Janet Kholowa and Klaus Fiedler, *In the Beginning God Created them Equal*
--, *Mtumwi Paulo ndi Udindo wa Amayi Mumpingo*
--, *Pachiyambi Anawalenga Chimodzimodzi*
Harry Langworthy, *'Africa for the African' – The Life of Joseph Booth*
Ian and Jane Linden, *Catholics, Peasants and Chewa Resistance* (reprint)
Patrick Makondesa, *Moyo ndi Utumiki wa Mbusa ndi Mai Muocha wa Providence Industrial Mission*
John McCracken, *Politics and Christianity in Malawi 1975-1940: The Impact of the Livingstonia Mission on the Northern Province*
Hilary Mijoga, *The Pauline Notion of Deeds of the Law*
Owen Mkandawire, *Chiswakhata Mkandawire of Livingstonia*
Fulata Moyo and Martin Ott, *Christianity and the Environment*

David Mphande, *Nthanthi za Chitonga za Kusambizgiya ndi Kutauliya*
Stephen Kauta Msiska, *Golden Buttons: Christianity and Traditional Religion among the Tumbuka*
Augustinus Musopole, *Being Human in Africa*
Yesaya Zerenji Mwase, *Essential and Paramount Reasons for Working Independently*
Silas S. Ncozana, *The Spirit Dimensions in African Christianity : A Pastoral Study Among the Tumbuka People of Northern Malawi*
--, *Sangaya : A Leader in the Synod of Blantyre*
--, *Sangaya : Mtsogoleri wa Sinodi ya Blantyre : Mpingo wa CCAP*
M.S. Nzunda, Kenneth R. Ross (eds), *Church, Law and Political Transition in Malawi*
Patrick O'Malley, *Living Dangerously: A Memoir of Political Change in Malawi*
Peggy Owen (ed.), *When Maize and Tobacco are not Enough: A Church Study of Malawi's Agro-Economy*
Martin Ott, Kings M. Phiri, Nandini Patel (eds), *Malawi's Second Democratic Elections: Process, Problems and Prospects*
Martin Ott, *Theology in Images*
Martin Pauw, *From Mission to Church: The History of Nkhoma Synod of the C.C.A.P. 1889-1968*
Isabel Apawo Phiri, *Women, Presbyterianism, and Patriarchy*
Kings M. Phiri, Kenneth R. Ross (eds), *Democratization in Malawi: A Stocktaking*
Hubert Reijnaerts, Ann Nielsen, Matthew Schoffeleers, *Montfortians in Malawi: Their Spiritual and Pastoral Approach*
Edwin D. Roels and others, *Mayankho Odalirika – Answers to Live By* (bilingual; ed. Steven Paas)
Andrew C. Ross, *Blantyre Mission and the Making of Modern Malawi*
Kenneth R. Ross, *Church, University and Theological Education in Malawi*
--, *Gospel Ferment in Malawi: Theological Essays*
--, (ed.), *Christianity in Malawi: A Source Book*
--, (ed.), *Faith at the Frontiers of Knowledge*
--, (ed.), *God, People and Power in Malawi: Democratization in Theological Perspective*
--, *Here Comes Your King: Christ, Church and Nation in Malawi*
Matthew J. Schoffeleers, *Guardians of the Land*
--, *In Search of Truth and Justice*
--, *Religion and the Dramatisation of Life: Spiritual Beliefs and Rituals in Southern and Central Malawi*
George Shepperson, Thomas Price, *Independent African: John Chilembwe and the Nyasaland Rising*
Boston Soko, with Gerhard Kubik, *Nchimi Chikanga: The Battle Against Witchcraft in Malawi*
Boston Soko, *Chikanga: A Traditional Healer*
T.Jack Thompson, *Touching the Heart: Xhosa Missionaries to Malawi*
Zacharias Ursinus and Caspar Olevianus, *Katekisma wa Heidelberg – Heidelberg Catechism* (bilingual; ed. Steven Paas)
Ernst R. Wendland, *Bukhu Loyera: An Introduction to the New Chichewa Translation*
--, *Preaching that Grabs the Heart: A Rhetorical-Stylistic Study of the Chichewa Revival Sermons of Shadrack Wame*

Kachere Series Editors: J.C. Chakanza, F.L. Chingota, Klaus Fiedler, P.A. Kalilombe, S. Mahomed, Fulata Moyo, Martin Ott; For Mvunguti Books also: Saidi Chiphangwi, Joel Manda, Silas Nyirenda

www.ingramcontent.com/pod-product-compliance
Lightning Source LLC
Chambersburg PA
CBHW021146230426
43667CB00005B/279